D0753283

FIRST NATIONS OF NORTH AMERICA

ARCTIC PEOPLES

Robin S. Doak

HEINEMANN LIBRARY
CHICAGO, ILLINOIS

www.heinemannraintree.com
Visit our website to find out
more information about
Heinemann-Raintree books.

To order:
☎ Phone 888-454-2279
🖥 Visit www.heinemannraintree.com
to browse our catalog and order online.

Original illustrations © Capstone Global Library, Ltd.
Illustrated by Mapping Specialists, Ltd.
Originated by Capstone Global Library, Ltd.
Printed in China by China Translation and Printing Services

14 13 12
10 9 8 7 6 5 4 3 2

Library of Congress Cataloging-in-Publication Data
Doak, Robin S. (Robin Santos), 1963-
  Arctic peoples / Robin S. Doak.
    p. cm.—(First Nations of North America)
  Includes bibliographical references and index.
  ISBN 978-1-4329-4945-7 (hc)—
ISBN 978-1-4329-4956-3 (pb) 1. Inuit—Juvenile literature. 2.
Eskimos—Juvenile literature. 3. Aleuts—Juvenile literature. 4.
Arctic regions—Juvenile literature. I. Title.
  E99.E7D53 2012
  971.9004'9712—dc22   2010040604

Acknowledgments

The author and publisher are grateful to the following
for permission to reproduce copyright material: Corbis:
pp. 31 (© Corbis), 35 (© Bettmann); Getty Images: pp. 37
(Win McNamee), 41 (AFP PHOTO/GEOFF ROBINS);
Library of Congress Prints and Photographs Division: pp.
4, 12, 13, 15, 16, 18, 19, 23, 26, 28, 36; National Geographic
Stock: pp. 5 (GORDON WILTSIE), 10 (PETE RYAN), 33
(ALASKA STOCK IMAGES), 38 (NICHOLAS DEVORE
III); Nativestock.com: pp. 11 (© Marilyn Angel Wynn), 14
(© Marilyn Angel Wynn), 17 (© Marilyn Angel Wynn);
Photolibrary: pp. 22 (ALASKA STOCK IMAGES/© Chris
Arend), 25 (© Ton Koene), 29 (© Steven Kazlowski);
Shutterstock: p. 39 (© Fernando Jose Vasconcelos Soares);
The Bridgeman Art Library International: p 32 (© National
Museums of Scotland); The Granger Collection: pp. 20, 21, 24.

Cover photograph of a seal mask from the Yup'ik culture
reproduced with permission from Art Resource, NY (Mingei
International Museum).

We would like to thank Peter Collings, Ph.D., for his invaluable
help in the preparation of this book.

Every effort has been made to contact copyright holders of
any material reproduced in this book. Any omissions will
be rectified in subsequent printings if notice is given to
the publisher.

All the Internet addresses (URLs) given in this book were valid
at the time of going to press. However, due to the dynamic
nature of the Internet, some addresses may have changed, or
sites may have changed or ceased to exist since publication.
While the author and publisher regret any inconvenience this
may cause readers, no responsibility for any such changes can
be accepted by either the author or the publisher.

Contents

Some words are shown in bold **like this**. You can find out what they mean by looking in the glossary.

Who Were the First People in North America?

In 1830 Scottish adventurer John Ross explored the icy Arctic region of North America. He thought the **polar** area was a harsh, wild, unlivable place. But he was astonished to find people thriving in this **desolate** region. He wrote in his journal that the people living in this unwelcoming area had everything they needed to survive.

People **inhabited** North America for hundreds of years before the arrival of European settlers and adventurers. They covered every region of the continent, from the northernmost polar reaches to the hot, steamy tropical areas in the South. Today, **descendants** of these first peoples continue to live throughout the continent. They carry on many of the traditions and customs handed down through the centuries.

▶ The Arctic is one of the harshest, most desolate **ecosystems** on Earth. It has been called a frozen desert because it receives such little **precipitation**.

▲ The first people to live in the Arctic adapted their homes, clothing, and diet to survive and thrive in the frigid region.

American Indian and Native American

When Christopher Columbus arrived in the Americas in 1492, he believed he had found Asia, known then as the Indies. He called the people who were living in the region "Indians." For centuries, all of the first peoples of the Americas were known as Indians.

In the late 1900s, people began to use the term "Native Americans." Later, the term "American Indians" came into use. There is no agreement among these peoples as to what is the correct term. Native peoples in the Arctic prefer to refer to themselves by their place of residence or origin, such as, "I am an Aleut."

How the first people came to North America

Scientists believe that the **ancestors** of today's American Indians came to North America thousands of years ago during the last **Ice Age**. They traveled over the Bering Land Bridge, a thousand-mile stretch of land that connected Asia to North America. These early travelers were most likely hunters, following **migrating** herds of animals such as mammoths and reindeer.

The new arrivals, known today as **Paleo-Indians**, spread throughout North America. Some traveled south, heading into present-day Mexico and beyond. Other groups made their homes on the plains, hunting buffalo.

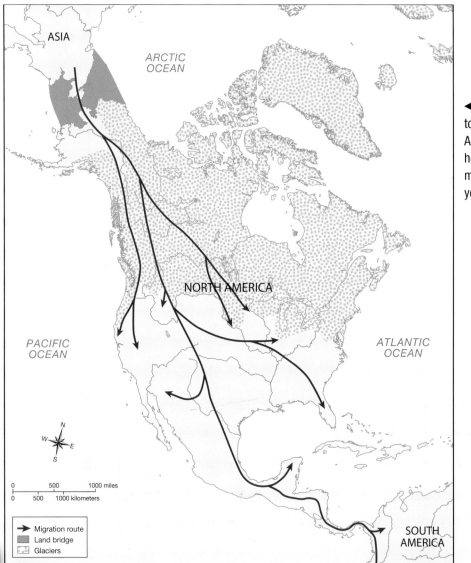

◄ The first people to live in North America migrated here from Asia more than 12,000 years ago.

The climate and geography of where people settled affected how they adapted to life in their new homes.

Still others settled on the east and west coasts of the continent, becoming farmers and growing crops such as squash, corn, and beans.

End of the land bridge

Scientists think that the last people to travel over the land bridge remained in the cold, harsh Arctic region. These people settled in northwestern Alaska between 6,000 and 7,000 years ago, then spread east across Canada. Some traveled as far as Greenland.

As the last Ice Age ended, temperatures warmed. Glaciers melted and ocean levels rose. The Bering Land Bridge eventually disappeared, and the migration of people, animals, and plants came to an end.

Who Are the Arctic Peoples?

To survive in their new homes, many of the first **inhabitants** of North America joined together in different groups, forming hundreds of tribes and nations. Each tribe shared a common language, religious beliefs, and customs.

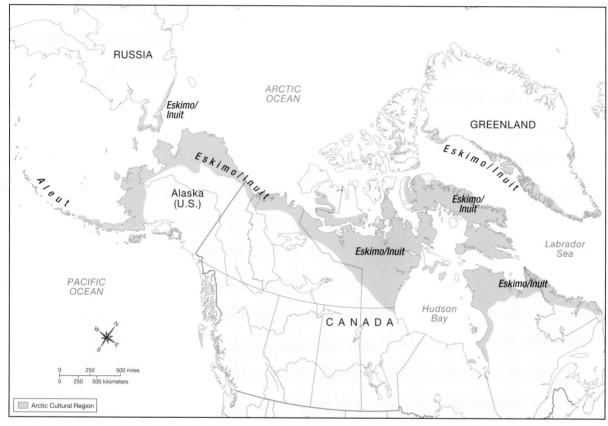

▲ The original people of North America spread throughout the continent. They even settled in one of its harshest environments—the Arctic.

Peoples of the Arctic

In the Arctic, there are two major groups of people—the **Eskimo** and the **Aleut**. Eskimo groups include the Yup'ik and Inupiat in Alaska, the **Inuit** and Inuvialuit in Canada, and the Kalaallit in Greenland. Before European contact, historians estimate that there were about 16,000 Eskimos living in Alaska.

The Aleuts, who are closely related to the Eskimo, live on the Aleutian Islands off the southern coast of Alaska. Aleut groups include the Unangax and Alutiiq (Sugpiaq).

The largest group of Arctic peoples is the Inuit of **polar** Canada and Greenland. Siberian Eskimos in Russia are closely related to the Yup'ik.

LANGUAGE

Eskimo and Inuit

In the 1500s, the first Europeans to meet the peoples of the Arctic called them Eskimo. The word "Eskimo" is thought to have come from a term used by the early peoples of Quebec, Canada, meaning "snowshoe netter." American Indians who spoke Algonquin called the polar peoples by a similar word which meant "eater of raw flesh."

In Canada, Arctic peoples do not like to be called Eskimo. Many people there find that term offensive. They prefer "Inuit," which means "people" in the Inuit language.

The Arctic

The Arctic region, which covers more than 11 million acres (4.5 million hectares), is one of the harshest on Earth. For nine months out of the year, winter holds the region in its icy grip. In the deepest winter, the Sun doesn't shine and temperatures can drop to -60°F (-51°C). The ground is frozen solid and covered with ice and snow.

The people of the Arctic have **adapted** to the cycle of the seasons. They prepare for the harsh winter by hunting, fishing, and **preserving** food during the spring, summer, and fall.

▲ The Arctic environment is one of the most challenging on Earth, yet people have been living there comfortably for thousands of years, including Resolute Bay, Nunavut, Canada, shown here.

Seasons in the Arctic

During the Arctic winter, food is difficult to find. Many whales, seals, and birds have **migrated** to warmer regions. Other animals hibernate during the long winter. A human without the proper clothing, supplies, and knowledge of how to survive in this frigid **ecosystem** would die in very little time.

The Sun returns for the short, cool Arctic summer. Temperatures heat up to around 50°F (10°C) during July, the warmest month. The environment comes back to life. Moss, ferns, and flowering plants cover the Arctic **tundra**. Birds return to the area, and animals come out of hibernation. The Arctic is home to dozens of bird species, as well as about 40 land mammals, including moose, polar bears, and caribou. The oceans are also filled with life, including fish, seals, walruses, and whales.

▲ The peoples of the Arctic developed unique tools, homes, and clothing that allowed them to survive winters in the Arctic.

How Did Early Peoples Survive in the Arctic?

The first people to arrive in the Arctic quickly learned that, in order to survive, they must **adapt** to their new surroundings. They created tools, built homes, and made clothing that allowed them to make the most of the natural resources the **polar** region had to offer. They learned to hunt caribou, seals, and whales.

To improve their chances of survival, these first people banded together in small groups. They created small villages, made up of between 20 and 200 people. The people within each village were usually families that were related to one another.

▶ Just as it is today, the family was the most important unit in the early Arctic society. Each member played an important role.

▲ Most early Arctic villages were small and made up of people related to one another. The same is true today.

Family roles

The family was the most important part of early Arctic life. Each family member played an important role. The head of the family was the father, who hunted for food and built the family's homes. The oldest and most experienced male hunter often served as the head of the village as well. Other village members looked to him for wisdom and guidance.

Women played a key part in helping the family survive. They prepared food and made animal skins into tents and clothing. Even children had a role, collecting driftwood as well as herbs, greens, and berries to eat.

Early Arctic homes

To build their homes, the early peoples of the Arctic used the resources that were available to them. Because there were no trees, wood could not be used. Instead, the people built their homes of snow, dirt, whalebone, and animal hides.

In the winter, the **Aleut** people built sod homes called **barabaras**. These rectangular homes were dug into the dirt and surrounded by a frame of whalebone and driftwood. Then they were covered with a roof of sod and grass. In early *barabara* homes, people entered through a door in the roof. They climbed down a ladder to the main room. Some Arctic people lived in sod houses year-round.

Another type of Arctic home was the **igloo**. Although it was often used as a temporary hunting shelter, **Inuit** in the central Arctic lived in igloos throughout the winter. Igloos were dome-shaped structures built out of rectangular blocks of snow and ice.

▲ Sod houses, built partially into the earth, protected Arctic people from the freezing Arctic winds.

▲ An Inuit family sits in front of a **tupik**. Seals and furs hang off the home to dry.

Igloos

The word "igloo" has come to mean a domed house made out of ice and snow. But the Inuit word, *iglu*, means any type of home made out of any material.

Summer camps and blubber lamps

In the summer, the Arctic peoples traveled to summer camps close to the coast in order to fish and hunt. Here, they lived in tents called *tupiks*. The tents were made out of animal skins draped over whalebone or driftwood.

Lamps fueled with **blubber** or animal oil were an important item in native homes. These lamps gave off heat and light, and were used for cooking. Women were in charge of tending the oil lamps. Other household items included cooking pots, baskets, and tools.

How Did Early Arctic Peoples Hunt for Food?

In the Arctic, the ground is constantly covered with a layer of permafrost, ground that is permanently frozen. This makes growing crops impossible. Early Arctic peoples **adapted** over time to survive on a high-protein diet rich in animal meat and **blubber**, or fat from seals and whales. The native word for a meal of frozen whale skin and blubber is **muktuk**.

Hunting sea animals was the most important activity in Arctic life. Seal hunting took place year-round. The best time for hunting was when the days turned colder and the ice fields began to freeze up again. Whale hunting usually took place in the spring and the fall.

▲ Small **igloos** built on the ice were used by early Arctic peoples as temporary shelters when they hunted.

Hunting seals

Over centuries, Arctic peoples invented tools that improved their chances of catching the food their families needed to survive. They invented special ice drills, harpoons, knives, and spears. They created three-pronged tools called scratchers to attract seals with the sound of claws scraping on ice. All of these tools were crafted from **ivory** or bone.

Skill and patience were needed to hunt seals. First, hunters had to locate the breathing holes in the ice that seals used to get air before diving. Next, hunters might drill four holes around a breathing hole. A net, attached to the four holes, was lowered into the breathing hole. When the seal dived back into the water after coming up for air, it became tangled in the net.

▲ Arctic hunters made spears, harpoons, and scratchers from whalebone.

▲ Women **preserved** fish by hanging them in the Sun to dry. The fish needed to last through the upcoming winter.

Other food sources

The sea was the main food source for early Arctic peoples. In addition to hunting seals and whales, early peoples used nets and spears to catch fish. Early Arctic peoples also hunted and trapped land animals, including caribou and **polar** bears. They hunted fox and other small mammals with spring traps that were baited with blubber.

Everyone helps in the Arctic

Women and children took part in finding food for their families. They gathered eggs from wild birds and hunted ducks with weapons called **bolas**. The weapon is thrown through the air to hit and kill birds. Women and children also gathered berries and wild greens during the summer.

Women cut up and prepared the animals their husbands brought home. They had their own special knives, called **ulus**, to help them. They used the ulu to scrape and clean skins, to cut fish and chop up food, and even to cut hair.

Nothing goes to waste

Early Arctic peoples used every part of an animal. Nothing was wasted. Flesh, blubber, organs, and flippers were used for food. Skins and hides were used to cover **kayaks** and make tents and clothing. Animal bones and teeth were turned into clubs and fishhooks. Stomachs and intestines were used to make containers and clothing. Even an animal's **sinews** were used as thread for sewing clothing and other items.

▲ Arctic hunters used bows and arrows to hunt polar bears, caribou, and other animals.

How Did Early Arctic Peoples Get from Place to Place?

When hunting seals and other sea creatures, the early peoples of the Arctic used two different styles of boats—**kayaks** and **umiaks**.

Kayaks

Kayaks are lightweight, narrow boats constructed from whalebone and covered with seal hide. The kayak has a small opening in the top center for the hunter to sit in.

▲ An Arctic hunter in a kayak prepares to harpoon a seal.

Umiaks

Umiaks were larger than kayaks, and were completely open. These boats could carry as many as 20 people at a time. They were used to carry goods from one place to another. Men also used them for hunting whales.

Snowshoes and sleds

Most travel was done on foot. Arctic peoples used snowshoes to make traveling across the **tundra** easier. Snowshoes were oval or triangular in shape, and made of bone frames and hide straps.

To carry their goods back and forth between winter and summer camps, Arctic peoples built low, lightweight sleds. Some sled runners were made of whalebone. Others were made of strips of sealskin that were sewn together and stuffed with moss and dirt. Water was poured over the strips, which then froze and became hard as rock.

Some sleds were pulled by people, but others were pulled by teams of dogs. Arctic peoples **bred** and cared for malamutes, Siberian huskies, and **Inuit** sled dogs. The dogs also helped the Arctic peoples hunt by finding seal holes and animals.

▲ Early Arctic peoples built toboggans by lashing strips of whalebone together.

What Types of Clothing Did Early Arctic Peoples Wear?

The early peoples of the Arctic created special clothes that were well suited for life in the North. They used the animals they hunted to make warm, comfortable clothing that offered protection from the weather. They made robes and other garments using sealskins and caribou hides. The fur of foxes, rabbits, and wolves was also used. They invented the first down-filled clothing by stuffing bird feathers into coats.

Arctic peoples made pants out of animal hides. They made these pants by sewing together leggings for the fronts and backs of the legs. Pants provided more warmth and greater protection than fur or leather leggings. Some historians believe Arctic peoples may even have invented long underwear.

▲ **Aleut** people added decorations and color to their everyday clothing. Arctic people today carry on this tradition.

Although native clothes were always functional, they could also be very beautiful. Aleuts wore cone-shaped wooden hats with figures painted on them. Aleut men and women wore clothes with animal teeth, beads, and **ivory** decorations sewn on. Jackets might be decorated with bird feathers.

Jewelry, tattoos, and piercings

Women and men decorated their bodies, too. Women wore jewelry made out of bones and beads. Men and women tattooed their faces, hands, legs, and arms. In some groups, men wore bones or pins of ivory through holes in their cheeks and noses. They also used plugs of ivory to pierce their lower lips. These plugs, called **labrets**, were considered a mark of manhood. Today, Arctic people carry on some of these traditions.

▶ Arctic peoples developed clothing suited to their environment.

23

▲ The kayak becomes watertight when the hunter fastens his special coat, used for hunting, around the opening of the boat.

Special clothes for hunting

Early Arctic hunters needed to have special clothing to keep them warm and dry, especially during the cold winter months. When outside, all parts of the body had to be covered. Exposure of any skin could lead to frostbite or a condition called **hypothermia**, which can cause death.

Parkas

One important garment was the **parka**. The parka was a loose-fitting, hooded coat made of caribou hide or sealskin. Some parkas fell to the thigh, while others went down to the ankles. Winter parkas had two fur-lined layers for extra warmth.

Parkas made of sealskins were essential when hunting whale or seal. Sealskin is waterproof and light. Seal oil was rubbed on the parka to make it even more waterproof.

Boots

Boots were another important piece of hunting gear. Called **mukluks**, these boots were made with sealskin and oiled for extra protection against water. Arctic women used the flippers of sea lions for the shoes' bottoms. The flippers gripped the ice and prevented slipping and skidding. In other areas, pieces of bone or ivory were attached to the bottom of the boots for the same purpose. The insides of the boots were lined with moss to keep them dry.

Snow Goggles

Early Arctic peoples quickly learned that the glare of sunshine on ice and snow was blinding. They created snow goggles made out of wood and ivory. These carved masks tied at the back of the head with **sinew** or straps of hide. There were small eye slits to look through.

▲ A young Arctic boy wears a pair of carved snow goggles to protect his eyes.

What Did Early Arctic Peoples Believe?

Early Arctic peoples believed that all things, whether human, animal, or object, had a spirit. These spirits could be good or bad, happy or upset. It was the job of the spiritual leader to communicate with the spirits and to learn what they wanted.

▲ The spiritual leader's mask was based on images he or she saw in his or her dreams.

The spiritual leader could be a man or woman. He or she was there to chase away evil spirits and to get the advice of helpful spirits. If the village hunters were not successful, the spiritual leader might be asked to find out what the spirits needed.

The spiritual leader, who was also the village healer, led ceremonies and rituals. During the ceremonies, the spiritual leader wore a mask. Chanting, singing, dancing, and drumming were all parts of these rituals.

Thanking animals

The early peoples of the Arctic believed that animals would not allow themselves to be captured and killed if they were not treated with respect. After a successful hunt, the hunter thanked the seal for giving itself up for food.

STORIES AND LEGENDS

The Story of Sedna

The story of Sedna is an **Inuit** legend. When Sedna was a small girl, her angry father threw her into the sea. As she clung to the side of the boat, her father chopped off her fingers one by one. As the fingers touched the water, they turned into seals, whales, and other sea animals. Sedna sank to the bottom, where she lives today and commands all sea creatures.

How Did Early Arctic Peoples Pass the Long Winters?

In the winter, when the Sun doesn't rise, early Arctic peoples had plenty to do to keep busy. Much of the wintertime activity was aimed at preparing for the coming hunting season. Women repaired worn clothing and sewed new garments. Men repaired their weapons and hunting equipment. They carved new gear out of **ivory** or bone.

Winter was also the perfect time for families to sit together and tell stories and sing songs. Storytelling was an important art among the early Arctic peoples. This was how village and family history, traditions, and customs were passed on to the next **generation**.

▲ For adults, winter was the time to repair hunting equipment. Children played with toys made from bones, ivory, and animal hide.

Ceremonies and celebrations

Many important ceremonies were held during the wintertime. One such ceremony was the Yup'ik Bladder Festival. During this festival, the bladders of the hunted seals were hung in the men's house. For five days, the people would celebrate and thank the souls of the seals living in the bladders. Then they would throw the bladders into the sea, hoping that the seals would be reborn.

Villages sometimes invited neighboring groups to their festivals. For the **Aleuts**, such visits were a chance for friendly competition. The men, women, and children dressed in their best clothes, and dances were held inside the large communal building. Men from each village wrestled against one another. They held singing and storytelling contests. Modern Arctic people carry on these ceremonies and celebrations.

▶ In the spring, Arctic people in Alaska celebrate successful whaling with the blanket festival, which involves playing the blanket toss game.

A Day in the Life of an Early Inuit Child

For an **Inuit** boy, daily life is all about learning to survive and help his family. There are no schools for the boy to attend. Instead, he learns everything he needs to know by listening and watching. He listens to his parents tell stories of hunting, fishing, and survival. He watches as his father makes repairs to the family's **igloo** and carves a small figure out of **ivory**.

The boy also learns by playing. When he was younger, he had tops and pickup sticks made from ivory. He also had a yo-yo made from seal hide. These toys helped him improve his **dexterity** and **agility**. His sister has a doll made of animal hides. She learned how to sew by making clothes for the doll.

Today the boy will play with his friends in the village. They will run, wrestle, and lift weights. Later, they'll play a game of keep-away with a ball made out of caribou hide and stuffed with moss. Afterward, the boy will help his mother gather berries.

Tomorrow is an important day for the boy. For the first time, he will go on a seal hunt with his father. All of the stretching games and leg and hand massages over the past years have led up to this moment. He has thrown spears at targets and sat in one position for hours to prepare for harpooning and the long hunt. If the boy does well, he may soon be making his own hunting trips. Eventually, he will be ready to start to care for his own family.

▲ Games played by Inuit, **Eskimo**, and **Aleut** children helped prepare them to be adults.

What Kinds of Art and Music Do Arctic Peoples Create?

Arctic peoples are well known for their carving skills. In addition to tools, equipment, and weapons, they carved toys as well as animal and human figures out of tusks, bone, and stone. They also carved buttons, belt buckles, and jewelry. Some even carved tiny pictures on buttons and beads.

European and American whalers copied this form of native art. To pass the spare hours at sea, they carved pictures on whale teeth. This art became known as **scrimshaw**.

▶ **Inuit** people of Cape Dorset used modern tools to create beautiful carvings, such as this boy and seal.

Arctic music

Music was important to the people of the Arctic. They made handheld drums out of caribou hide and other animal skins stretched over bone or wood frames. The drum's handle was made out of bone or **ivory**, which was also used to make drumsticks. Drums were used at dances and ceremonies.

Early Arctic peoples also made rattles to use during ceremonies. The rattles were **puffin** beaks, bear claws, or other materials attached to a wooden frame. Sometimes the beaks and claws were sewn onto mittens.

ART AND CULTURE

Woven Baskets

Another native art form is woven baskets. In the past, **Aleut** people created baskets woven from sea grass. They collected the grass from the shore in the summertime. The grass was dyed by soaking it in seawater, then drying it in the Sun. Some early peoples dyed their baskets with berries that they found. Others made baskets out of baleen, the stiff, bone-like plates found in the mouths of some whales. Native baskets were beautiful and useful. They were used to carry fish and other goods. Today Arctic people still carry on the tradition of making baskets.

▶ Aleut women pass their skills as basket weavers from one **generation** to another.

How Did Arctic Peoples Interact with Other Peoples?

First contact between Arctic peoples and Europeans occurred in the 900s CE, when **Norse** settlers from Iceland landed in Greenland. These settlements disappeared by 1350. While there was conflict between the Norse and the **Inuit**, the settlements died out because of deteriorating climate.

In 1576 European explorers began mapping the Arctic in search of the **Northwest Passage**, a quick way from North America to Asia. The first such explorer was Martin Frobisher, who set sail from England in 1576. Frobisher explored the eastern Arctic and met Inuit peoples there.

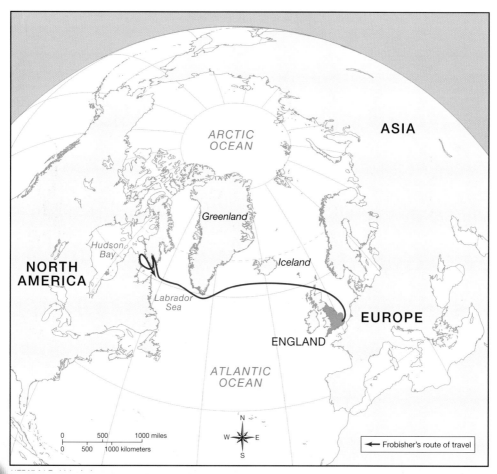

▲ This map shows Martin Frobisher's journey.

Fur hunters and whalers

In the 1780s, Russian fur hunters looking for otter, seal, and fox skins built **outposts** in the Aleutian Islands. The Russians killed many Arctic people and forced others to hunt for them. European and American fur hunters followed in the early 1800s.

In the mid-1800s, American whalers set up stations in the Arctic. The whalers traded with Arctic peoples, exchanging weapons for food and furs.

Disease

The hunters and whalers brought diseases such as **influenza**, **cholera**, and **measles** to the Arctic. Arctic peoples had no **resistance** to the diseases, and their populations were destroyed. Six out of ten **Eskimo** people died during the early 1900s. Diseases, such as tuberculosis, continued to affect the central Arctic until the 1960s.

▶ American Frederick Cook, pictured here, was just one explorer who hired Arctic men to help him find his way through the Arctic.

Missionaries bring change

In the 1850s, Christian **missionaries** followed traders and whalers into the Arctic. The missionaries wanted to **convert** Arctic peoples to their religion. They tried to help the Arctic peoples by offering them schooling and getting them to stop drinking alcohol. However, they would not allow the Arctic peoples to practice their traditional rituals or speak their native languages.

Arctic peoples faced increasing pressure to convert to nonnative society. Arctic children were forced to travel hundreds of miles from their homes to live at nonnative schools. Here, they were taught to speak English. If they spoke their own languages at school, they were punished. The 1960s and 1970s would bring an end to these practices.

▲ Before the mid-1900s, Arctic children attended schools in which they had to conform to nonnative ways.

▲ Arctic people are working to save the Arctic and stop global climate change by protesting oil drilling.

Working together for rights

Since the 1960s, Arctic Alaskans have come together to make sure their rights to maintain their own culture are honored. They are also fighting to **preserve** their land and hunting rights. In 1971 the Alaska Federation of Natives won a settlement of cash and land from the U.S. government. In 1977 the Alaska Eskimo Whaling Commission was formed to fight for Arctic peoples' right to hunt whales.

More recently, Arctic peoples are making their voices heard on the issue of oil drilling in Alaska. They say that this practice is disrupting native hunting and whaling. Arctic peoples have formed a group to try to stop any new oil, gas, or coal exploration in Alaska.

What Have Arctic Peoples Given to the World?

Arctic peoples have been contributing to European and American culture for hundreds of years. Upon first contact, they taught the earliest European explorers how to survive in the **polar** environment. The explorers copied native clothing and gear, including **parkas**, snowshoes, and goggles. American and Russian hunters and whalers also benefited from native knowledge about hunting. They borrowed native weapon and tool designs.

Today, we can see the influence of the first Arctic peoples in many places. Every winter, people wear feather-filled parkas in cold areas to keep warm. They head to the mountains to ski and toboggan, and use snowshoes to travel through snowy woods. In the summer, people use **kayaks** on lakes, oceans, and rivers. Today's kayaks are usually built with plastic and fiberglass.

▲ People all over the world use kayaks.

Contributions to science

Arctic knowledge has advanced modern science as well. Most scientific knowledge about the Arctic region, especially biology, has been built upon Arctic knowledge. Scientists are using modern equipment combined with **Inuit** knowledge to study weather and global climate change. Others are working with Arctic people to better understand the habits of animals in the Arctic environment.

▲ An Arctic guide shows an explorer how to survive in the Arctic by eating wild goose eggs.

LANGUAGE

Survival of Native Arctic Words

Arctic words survive in place names and items. The name "Alaska," for example, comes from the **Aleut** word *alaxsxa*, which means "Great Land." In recent years, Canada has been adopting more Inuit names for places that had once been renamed by English explorers and settlers. In addition, the words **"igloo"**, "kayak", and "anorak" (a kind of parka) are all native Arctic terms that have become part of everyday speech.

Where Are the Peoples of the Arctic Today?

Arctic peoples continue to live throughout the Arctic region. In Alaska, Arctic people make up about 15 percent of the total population. Most of these people live in Anchorage, Alaska's largest city.

In the western Arctic, the way Arctic people live has changed. Many Arctic men combine working jobs with traditional hunting activities. Arctic families live in modern homes with electricity, water, and televisions. They drive snowmobiles and all-terrain vehicles.

Nunavut

In the early 1970s, eastern Arctic people lobbied the Canadian government for their own land. In 1999 Canada granted them about 775,000 square miles (2 million square kilometers) of land in the Northwest Territories. Called Nunavut, or "Our Land," the region is a self-governing territory of Canada.

▲ Nunavut covers about one-fifth of the entire area of Canada.

▲ Iqaluit is the capital and largest city in Nunavut.

Today, nearly 32,000 people live in Nunavut's 26 communities. About 85 percent of all people who live there are **Inuit**. Life in the territory is not easy. Poverty, unemployment, and the cost of living are high. Nunavut's leaders are working hard to change things for the better.

BIOGRAPHY

Paul Okalik

Paul Okalik was born May 26, 1964, in the Northwest Territories. As a young man, Okalik took part in the negotiations to form the territory of Nunavut. When the territory was formed in 1999, Okalik was chosen to serve as its premier, or leader. He served in that position until November 2008. He continues to represent his region of Nunavut in the territorial assembly.

Timeline

about 10,000 BCE   People from Asia cross the Bering Land Bridge to North America.

about 5,000 BCE   The first people settle along what is now the Arctic cultural region.

900s CE   **Norse** settlers establish villages in Greenland.

about 1350   Norse settlements in Greenland die out.

1576   English explorer Martin Frobisher explores the eastern Arctic.

1780s   Russian fur hunters build outposts in the Aleutian Islands.

early 1800s   European and American fur hunters build stations in the Arctic.

1830   Scottish adventurer John Ross explores the Arctic region and records his meetings with the early Arctic peoples there.

mid-1800s   American whalers begin hunting off the coast of Alaska.

1850s   Christian **missionaries** arrive in the Arctic and begin converting Arctic peoples.

April 1908   American Explorer Frederick Cook claims to have reached the North Pole, with the help of two Arctic guides. His claim is later discredited.

early 1900s   Six out of ten Eskimos die from diseases brought by
               European and American visitors.

1971   The Alaska Federation of Natives wins a settlement of
        cash and land from the U.S. government.

1977   The Alaska Eskimo Whaling Commission is formed to
        fight for Arctic peoples' right to hunt whales.

1999   Nunavut is formed.

2005   Nunatsiavut, a territory occupied by Inuits in
        Newfoundland and Labrador, Canada, is formed.

Glossary

adapt to make suitable to or fit for a specific use or situation

agility the ability to move quickly

Aleut Arctic people of North America who live in the Aleutian Islands

ancestor a person from whom someone is descended, such as a grandparent

barabara sod home built by the Aleut people

blubber fat of seals, whales, and other sea mammals

bola weapon made of stones or ivory pieces tied to strips of animal hide straps

bred produced and raised young

cholera infectious, potentially deadly disease that affects the stomach and intestines

convert to convince someone to change from one religion to another

descendant a person born from a certain group or family

desolate dreary, deserted

dexterity physical skill

ecosystem an environment, along with the creatures living there

Eskimo Arctic peoples of North America who live in Alaska

generation group of people born within a certain time period

hypothermia condition in which the body temperature drops below normal

Ice Age one of several periods of cold temperatures in Earth's early history

igloo dome-shaped ice house built by the Arctic peoples

influenza contagious infection caused by a virus

inhabit to live in an area

Inuit Arctic people of North America who live in Canada and Greenland

ivory material that makes up the tusks of walruses

kayak narrow, lightweight boat built for one person; from the native word for "man's boat"

labret plug of ivory or bone that is inserted into holes in the lower lip

measles contagious disease caused by a virus

migrate move from one place to another

missionary a person who performs religious work, often in faraway places

mukluks boots worn by Arctic peoples

muktuk native word for blubber when eaten as a meal

Norse people of ancient Norway, Sweden, Denmark, or Iceland

Northwest Passage sea route from the Atlantic to the Pacific Ocean through North America

outpost a settlement in a far-off land

Paleo-Indians first people to live in the Arctic

parka warm, loose coat made of caribou hide or other material

precipitation rainfall or snowfall

preserve save or protect

polar of or near the north or south poles

puffin type of seabird that lives in the Arctic and other northern areas

resistance natural immunity or protection from disease

scrimshaw carving on whalebone or ivory

sinew tissue in the body that connects bone to muscle

tundra treeless plains in the Arctic

tupik tent used by Arctic peoples in the summertime

ulu special knife used by women to cut blubber and other items

umiak open boat used for hauling goods, whaling, or transportation; from the native word for "woman's boat"

Find Out More

Books

Ipellie, Alootook and David MacDonald. *The Inuit Thought of It: Amazing Arctic Innovations.* Buffalo, NY: Annick Press, 2007.

Rivera, Raquel. *Arctic Adventures: Tales from the Lives of Inuit Artists.* Toronto, Canada: Groundwood/House of Anansi Press, 2007.

Rudinger, Joel. *Sedna: Goddess of the Sea.* Huron, OH: Cambric Press, 2006.

Websites

Alaska Native Heritage Center
www.alaskanative.net
This is the home page of the Alaska Native Heritage Center.

Canadian Museum of Civilization
www.civilization.ca/splash.html
This home page of the Canadian Museum of Civilization, a national museum, highlights Canada's history.

Government of Nunavut
www.gov.nu.ca/
Here is the government site for the territory of Nunavut.

Indigenous Environmental Network: REDOIL
www.ienearth.org/redoil.html
Read information on REDOIL, the group fighting expansion of gas and oil exploration in the Alaskan Arctic.

National Park Service: Bering Land Bridge
www.nps.gov/bela/
Visit the National Park Service page to learn about the Bering Land Bridge National Preserve in Alaska.

DVDs

American Experience: Minik, the Lost Eskimo. DVD. Directed by Axel Engstfeld. PBS, 2008.

Great North. DVD. Directed by Martin J. Dignard and William Reeve. Razor, 2005.

Growing Up Arctic. DVD. Animal Planet, 2008.

Places to visit

Bering Land Bridge National Preserve
Seward Peninsula, AK
www.nps.gov/bela/index.htm

National Museum of the American Indian
National Mall
Washington, D.C.
www.nmai.si.edu/

Nunatta Sunakkutaangit Museum
Iqaluit, Nunavut, Canada
www.nunavuttourism.com/plan/operator.aspx?o=224&l=0,2,5

Further research

What parts of the Inuit or Eskimo lifestyle did you find the most interesting? How does life for people in the Arctic compare to the way native people live today in other regions? How did the people who first lived in your area contribute to life today? To learn more about the Arctic or other cultural regions, visit one of the suggested places or head to your local library for more information.

Index